M000188582

Tamales, Comadres
AND THE MEANING OF CIVILIZATION

secrets, recipes, history, anecdotes, and a lot of fun

Ellen Riojas Clark, Ph.D.
La mera mera tamalera

y su comadre

La tortillera y curandera
Carmen Tafolla, Ph.D.

San Antonio, Texas
2011

Tamales, Comadres, and the Meaning of Civilization © 2011
by Ellen Riojas Clark and Carmen Tafolla.

Designed by Thelma Ortíz Muraida

Printed Edition ISBN 978-0-916727-81-9
ePub ISBN 978-1-60940-132-0
Kindle ISBN 978-1-60940-133-7
Library PDF ISBN 978-1-60940-134-4

Published by
Wings Press
627 E. Guenther
San Antonio, Texas 78210
Phone/fax: (210) 271-7805

On-line catalogue and ordering:
www.wingspress.com
All Wings Press titles are distributed to the trade by
Independent Publishers Group
www.ipgbook.com
and in Europe by
www.gazellebookservices.co.uk

All rights reserved. No part of this book may be reproduced, except for brief excerpts for
critical and review purposes, without written permission of the authors.

In 2009, a smaller version of this work was printed in a limited edition
in support of the Guadalupe Cultural Arts Center.

Printed in China

COVER ART: "Tamales, Tamales, Tamales" (1998, acrylic and ground chile on tablecloth) by Rolando Briseño represents all of the tamales he found, tasted, touched, and researched in his travels throughout Mexico, in *mercados, cocinas,* and old and new texts. Whenever he came upon a new tamal he would buy two, one to eat and one to paint. A special pilgrimage to the Huasteca region found the *zacahuil,* the 3 foot long *tamalón* that Fray Bernardino de Sahagún mentions in his writings as having an entire chicken in its center. The word 'hua' means tamal and food in Mayan. Briseño reproduced glyphs and the ancient depictions of tamales from codices, and also painted a Mayan receptacle made especially for tamales with three separate indentations, for three different sauces. Some of these tamales are literally impressed on the tablecloth for the painting. This painting is from the series *Moctezuma's Table* which will be published as an art book of the same title by Texas A & M University Press in 2010.

To Olga Kauffman and Thelma Ortiz-Muraida,
true MTA's (Masters of Tamalada Art)
without whom the physical reality of this book would have never happened,
for they inspired the textual shucks,
gathered the monetary shucks,
shaped the layout shucks,
designed the visual shucks,
found the printing shucks,
and made this tamalito happen.

— E.R.C. & C.T.—

Welcome to our *cocina*
and to our *corazón*.
Join us as we explore the timeless
meaning of gathering together
with family and friends
to celebrate survival
and love.

TABLE OF CONTENTS

AW SHUCKS
TAMALE TIDBITS

INTRODUCING... CIVILIZATION!

✳ ✳ ✳ ✳ ✳ ✳ ✳ ✳ ✳ ✳ ✳ ✳

So what do tamales and comadres have to do with civilization? Everything! As you unwrap those delicious, steaming, freshly-made tamales, gift-wrapped in corn shucks, that have kept human beings alive for more than seven thousand years on this continent, think about the things that last beyond nations, beyond languages, beyond flags. Our history and our stories are wrapped in those shucks, and our memories are wrapped in their love.

As a gift to all of you who ever dipped your hands in the magic masa, or who ever tasted its miraculous results, we three *comadres*—Ellen, Carmen, and Thelma—bring you this *tamalada* of touching stories and hilarious mishaps, hints, secrets, jokes, recipes, poems, blogs, and celebrity quotes—as pieces of our history and pieces of our hearts.

This book can best be described as a collaborative labor of love, which, just like a tamalada, requires laughter, tears, *chisme*, an intense amount of work, and a sense of wanting to feed a whole pueblo hungry to read about their culinary and historical *hojas*. It is a symbol of the giving our mothers and grandmothers did to feed us physically and spiritually. And if you wonder how this book came about, it was, very fittingly, out of that same sense of crazy *comadrazgo* and caring for the *comunidad*.

Ellen had spent 40 years hosting *tamaladas* at her house (see En Casa con Ellen, p. 12) and wanted to do something to honor her *tías*, her ancestors, and her descendents. Carmen wanted to do something to help her *comadre* Ellen be recognized for this work of cultural preservation and celebration, and to help her *cultura* document its cultural treasures, Thelma wanted to visually translate Carmen and Ellen's literary work into the format it deserved, to reflect the tablecloths and the *hojas*, and the celebration, the warmth, and smiles of *tamaladas*. And all three *comadres* wanted to benefit a community institution that has long celebrated the arts of San Antonio's West Side—the Guadalupe Cultural Arts Center. So, totally without any re-payment for their intense *tamalada*-type labor, in November of 2009, they decided to donate all proceeds from the first limited edition to the GCAC. The entire book was written, assembled, designed, "proposaled", funded, edited, and printed within four miraculous weeks of four comadres working late into the night, as Olga Kauffmann researched, prepared for and landed the generous donation of Valerie Gonzales, CEO of Delicious Tamales.

As if this wasn't enough of a miracle, Ellen talked Rolando Briseño into lending us his brilliant illustration *Tamales, Tamales* (see Cover Art credit on copyright page) and we leaned on the help of many a San Antonio genius (Robert Flynn, Antonia Castañeda, and Cary Clack, to name a few...) to pull together a book that truly represented the human aspect of tamales and tamale-making. In the process, we garnered everyone's favorite story or favorite tamal, including the memories and magic moments from Vicky Carr and Arturo Sandoval to El Curro, the Krayolas, Sandra Cisneros and Hints from Heloise!

The books, like a batch of steaming hot tamales, were finally ready on December 18, 2009 and, like any good batch of tamales, they disappeared! Within three days, the books were sold out! People bought five or six at a time, or a dozen—to send off to Missouri or Wisconsin or to their grand-mother in El Paso! People searched everywhere for copies, and one person reported finding theirs at an obscure raspa stand in West Texas! So, Wings Press came to the rescue and promised to bring to *el pueblo* and the world this much expanded trade edition.

May you unwrap these *hojas* with pleasure and the humbling awareness that they hold within them all the fun and flavor of 7,000 years of history... and all the meaning of civilization!

Top row: Gregg Barrios; Ya Ya & her girls; Carmen, Ernesto and Israel. Second row: Tamalada at Starpatch. Third row: Peter Falcon, Gertrude Baker, Big Sam, Erica.

EN CASA CON ELLEN

✳ ✳ ✳ ✳ ✳ ✳ ✳ ✳ ✳ ✳ ✳ ✳

Welcome to one of my Christmas *Tamaladas* to learn how to make this traditional favorite. I have been making tamales for over 40 years with family and friends at *Starpatch*, our home here in San Antonio. Though my mother, a wonderful and fancy cook, never made tamales, I did learn from a wonderful set of aunts. It was a childhood tradition to go over to my Dad's family home on Mistletoe Avenue for Open House on Christmas Eve for tamales and my favorite pecan refrigerator cookies.

Now, everyone comes to our home—our daughters, their friends, my granddaughters, my sister, her son Javier and his family, in-laws, elementary school friends, artists, students, colleagues, and people I don't even know. It seems like, over the years, everyone has participated at one time or the other! People bring their pots and take their tamales home to cook. Tamales are made in all sizes from Janet Purdy's one pounders to my mother's tiny *esquisitos*. Contests are held when there is still too much masa left and fatigue is setting in: who can makes them the fastest, the prettiest or the worst like Pam McCollum, a specialist in tamales/*pastelitos Puerto Ricanos*.

One year, Jennifer, our engineer daughter tried to inject an efficiency system into our *tamalada*. Everyone was assessed for abilities, my kitchen table became the workspace, everyone rotated every 20 minutes, talking was held to a minimum, and no drinking was allowed, though music was played. It was the only time the *masa* equaled the meat, the tamales were uniform, and the kitchen was spotless. But *el chiste de la tamalada* suffered.

Everyone comes to help make tamales, to learn about them, eat them, sing, gossip, cry, dance, drink, and to eat some more. We crown a *Reina de los Tamales* with the most elaborately regal *hoja* crown, made by Lisa Anaya's aunt, and we dance and sing around the first *olla de tamales*. Yes, dancing and singing DOES help to make them the fluffiest, spiciest, and best tamales ever. Don't forget to wear your best apron, put on your reddest lipstick and your longest earrings for, as my 96-year-old Tía Hope says, you have to respect the making of tamales.

Opening this book brings to you not only a collection of my very own recipes but highlights historical events, *cuentos* from people in our city and from afar, some famous, others infamous, and dances down many different paths to make you laugh and sing while you learn. *Disfruten.*

> "Make Tamales, not War."
> —Luz-María Prieto, community activist & former ACCD Trustee

ODE TO THE TAMAL

by Lisa Anaya (2004)

Oh, tamal,
of the golden corn husk,
of the savory meat,
of the most delicious & balanced *masa*.
Oh, tamal,
of the glorious corn field,
wavy with green stalks
and fresh corn.
Oh, tamal,
remember our loving, *chismosa* hands and
embrace the heat of the oven.
Oh, tamal,
cook *perfectamente bien*
so that you may melt
our palates and
warm our hearts.

ART, LABOR, AND THE GENIUS OF WOMEN:
A SHORT HISTORY OF TAMALES

by Antonia Castañeda, Ph.D., historian

Tamales, the ingenious creation of Indigenous women, originated in Mexico and Central America, possibly as early 7000 BCE; initially they were made of *teocintle*, the ancestor of modern maize, which grew wild and took considerable time to gather, grind, and process into *masa*. Making tamales was, and is, labor intensive! As no history is complete without understanding the words and meaning involved, let's take a closer look at the terminology of tamales, beginning with *teocintle*.

In Nahuatl, the language of the Mexica-Azteca and other indigenous peoples of Meso America, *teo* means god and *cintle*, is maize/corn. Teocintle is the God of Maize while Chicomecoatl is the Goddess of Maize.[1] Corn, then, is sacred. Before discussing tamales as sacred food, it is important to know that the term *tamal*, and its plural form *tamales*, are the Hispanized forms of the Nahuatl word *nixtamalli*, a compound of *nixtli*, meaning ashes, and *tamalli*, meaning unformed corn dough. Nixtamalization, a related term we do not often hear, is the ancient processing of field corn with wood ashes, though now we use *cal*, or slaked lime, to remove the hard skin around the kernel. This softens the corn for easier grinding, helps its digestibility, and increases the nutrients absorbed by the human body.[2] Since time immemorial, corn and its life cycle defined the cultural rhythms, the labors, the sacred rituals and the celebrations of Indigenous America.

Accordingly, in the *Popol Vuh*, the Mayan sacred book, the gods created people out of cornmeal, and thus the inhabitants of this land consider themselves people of corn.[3] Though each civilization has different creation stories, the Maya, the Mexica-Azteca, the Olmeca and the Tolteca all identified as people of corn.[4] Similarly, a creation story of the Huichol of the Sierra Madre Occidental, tells that Corn Mother presented her five daughters, each of whom symbolized one of the sacred colors of corn—white, red, yellow, molted, and blue—so that upon marrying the new race of humans, the latter could be nourished and would not perish.[5] We are nourished, and ingest our history, with every bite of a tamal!

Little did we know, when our mothers instructed us to clean the *hojas* still again, or to keep grinding corn in the *molino*, and to be cheerful about it *porque los tamales son sagrados* (because tamales are sacred) that tamales really were the sacred food of the gods. Historically, Indigenous women working collectively prepared countless varieties of delicious tamales for religious rites, festivals and celebrations to honor their gods. For Texcatlicpoca, the Jaguar God, Mexica-Azteca women prepared tamales of beans and chiles; of shrimp and chile for Huehueteotl, the Lord of Fire; and tamales of *huitlacotche*, served with cups of rich, frothy chocolate, for Tlaloc, the Lord of Rain and Thunder, whose rain they needed for corn and all other crops.[6] It is written that the varieties of tamales prepared for Moctezuma's court and ceremonial occasions included, among others, "tamales made of maize flowers with ground amaranth seed and cherries added. . . tamales stuffed with amaranth greens . . . tamales made with honey . . . white tamales with maize grains thrown in . . .

tamales of meat cooked with maize and yellow chiles; roast turkey hen and roast quail."[7] In tropical regions of Mexico, as well as in Central America, women wrap the *masa* in plantain/banana leaves instead of corn husks. Plantain leaf tamales are often square in shape, and can be large and thick. The term *Zacahuiles*, interestingly, is used in both Southern Tamaulipas and Northwestern Mexico to refer to very large tamales.

The varieties of tamales, whether made as offerings to the gods, for Moctezuma's court, or for family consumption, are infinite, as are our own individual, family, and community stories of making and eating tamales whether in the U.S., Mexico or any other part of the Americas. We know that in Texas, or "the land of the *Tejas*" as the Spanish chroniclers named it, the people of the Julimes and Jumano culture who lived at "*La Junta de los Rios Bravo y Concho*" cultivated and ate corn in one form or another at almost every meal.[8] In all probability, they also made tamales, which are a portable food and were historically used throughout the Americas to provision Indigenous armies, hunters, and travelers.[9] While we have yet to write a history of tamales in Texas, the small, slender tamal from the region of Monterrey, which may use either smooth or coarse dough and is made with shredded meat and red chiles, seems to predominate in South Texas.[10]

Tamales, then, are corn *delicacies*, savory corn packets if you will, consisting of deliciously prepared corn dough (*masa*) with or without a filling wrapped in a corn husk (*hoja para tamal*), and steam-cooked. The filling may be any kind of meat or seafood which has been cooked with herbs and spices, especially chile; but the

filling may also be fruits, seeds, beans, cheese or vegetables.

Across the millennia, tamales have been prepared and served to family, friends, and special guests during religious and other rites and communal celebrations. From the past to the present, the rich and varied history of tamales is embedded in the ancient art, labor, and genius of women.

◇◇

[1]   *Teocintle*. Corn plant, it is supposed to be the primitive corn (*Euclanea mexicana*). Etimology; Corn of god, teotl,god and *cintli*, corn. *Aztec Review: Nahuatl words incorporated into the Spanish language*, http://www.cambonli01.uuhost.uk.uu.net/forum/caribbean/bau/aztecwords.htm. Accessed November 20, 2009.

[2]   WikiTamale-Dictionary & Encyclopedia of Words and Terms Related to Tamales, http://www.thetexastamalewarehouse.com/wikitamale. Accessed, November 20, 2009.

[3]   Laura Carlsen, "The peole of corn: Maize is Mexico's lifeblood. . . ." *New Internationalist*, December, 2004, http://www.finarticles.com/p/articles/mi¬_m0JQP/is_374/ai_n8579640/. Accessed, November 20, 2009. For a children's book, see May Joan Gerson, People of *Corn: A Mayan Story* (New York: Little, Brown and Company, 1995).

[4]   "Tamale: Definition," http://www.answers.com/topic/tamal. Accessed, November 20, 2009.

[5]   "Evolución de teocintle hacia maíz mediada por cobre," *Laboratorio Químico de Productos Naturales*, http://www.qfb.umich.mx/investig.htm. Accessed November 20, 2009.

[6]   Jefffrey M. Pilcher, "*Que vivan los tamales!: Food and the Making of Mexican Identity* (Albuquerque: University of New Mexico Press, 1998).

[7]   Fray Bernardino de Sahagún, *General History of the Things of New Spain* (Florentine Codex), Vol.8, Kings and Lords, Part 9. Translated from the Nahuatl by Arthur J.D. Anderson and Charles Dibble. Santa Fe: Mongraphs of the School of American Research, No. 14 (School of American Research and the University of Utah, 1979).

[8]   María Eva Flores, D.C.P., and Julia Cauble Smith, "La Junta de Los Ríos," in The Handbook of Texas Online, http://tshaonline.org/handbook/online/articles/LL/ry11.html; Joe S. Graham, "Tex-Mex Foods," in The Handbook of Texas Online. http://www.tshaonline.org/handbook/online/articles/TT/lgtlt.htm. Accessed November 20, 2009.

[9]   "Tamale: Definition," http://www.answers.com/topic/tamal. Accessed, November 20, 2009.

[10]   "Mexican Tamales," http://www.gourtmetsleuth.com/tamales.htm. Accessed, November 2009.

CIVILIZATION Y LAS COMADRES

by Carmen Tafolla

****

*I*n the beginning, there were *tamales. . .*

Before the invention of the wheel, before the pyramids, before the Mayan zero, before the Fertile Crescent, *dos comadres* sat and worried about how folks were going to survive with so little civilization around them.

"You know, *comadre*, something's missing. I know, I know, we have caves and rocks, spears, animal skins, and even fires—ALL the conveniences —what more could we possibly want? But still... we need SOMETHING more—something on which to build complex social institutions, something deep and meaningful that inspires *familia* and *comunidad*. And... we need something creative too... something artistic."

"What's artistic mean?

"I don't know but I think it should look like—*hojas*, and, and maybe... at the center— hold the promise of a delicious *corazón*. Yeah, we need something alright, something that inspires higher thinking..."

"Like *chisme!*"

"And collaborative relationships..."

"Like *tamaladas!*"

"What's a *tamalada?*"

"I'm not sure, but it sounded good to me!"

"Here, *comadre*, put some corn on that *metate*. And, and, do we still have any venison left from yesterday?"

"Both? At the same time? But we only have two hands? If we're eating corn with one, and venison with the other, how will we grab the *chilpayates* when they wander too close to the fire? How will the hunters carry their spears and still be able to eat?"

"Grab that *hoja*, I got an idea...."

"*Hijole, comadre, tú con tus ideas!* I think that's why I like you!"

"What's 'like'?"

"I don't know. But let me hold your *chilpayate* in my *regazo* for you, so you can mess with that crazy idea and we can improve the way things work around here. The hunters are NEVER gonna do it, they're too busy channel-surfing for prey.

So they worked through the day and into the early hours of the evening, and when they were done, everyone came and gathered around their fire, and ate, and ate, and talked, and laughed, and one of the hunters said, "Hey, can I take some of those with me mañana when we head off to find meat? They fit real good in my hand."

"*Pos, pendejo*, why do you think we made'm?"

"*Pos*, whatever, you got the whole *palomilla* excited about it. Those little, what did you call'm, tamales, made a big hit, bigger than a big bang."

And that was the beginning of civilization, more than 9,000 years ago. Some scientists refer to it as The Big Bang Theory. *Las comadres* just call it... a *tamalada*.

Existentialism and Tamales
"Si el tamal está mal, no es tamal.
Si el tamal es tamal, no está mal."

How to Plot and Survive Your Very Own Tamalada

by Ellen Riojas Clark, *la gran tamalera*

Tamaladas have ALWAYS been labor-intensive, and have always bonded *familias* and friends closer together, in the realization that many hands can make any load lighter. *Pero ay Dios Mío*, the immensity of the work! The mere thought of making tamales make some women turn pale, shiver and run to buy them at Delicious Tamales! But this is the 21st century. There is much we can do to make a *Tamalada* easier.

Through the years, I have streamlined the process to make over 150 pounds of *masa* (plus fillings) into dozens and dozens of tamales every Christmas. I use traditional "*Mexica*" (Aztec) items such as *molcajetes, ollas, hojas,* and the timeless ingredients of corn, chile and, of course, the particular delicacies of the recipe. The recipe and the process have not changed since Pre-Columbian times. But I also use modern conveniences—such as my top-loading washing machine to soak my *hojas*, my heavy-duty mixer to make the *masa bien bofita* (fluffy), and the blender for the spices—to make it go faster. But knowing that *corazón*, spirit, and *sabor* are all about presentation, I dump the *masa* into my huge, huge, *cazuelas* and give it a good 10 minutes of *batiendo la masa* with my warm hands to give it that love and human touch.

After whirling the spices in the blender, I pour them into the *molcajete* to give that final grinding and to start the smells going in the kitchen. But, my most famous and time-saving technique of all is for soaking the darn *hojas*. If you don't know, *hojas* (dried corn shucks) are very dry and papery and have to be soft to create the best tamales. So, I do it with my washing machine! Not kidding, folks. First, I get rid of all the soap residue in the machine by running one cycle with only vinegar and water. Then, the night before the *tamalada*, I put the *hojas* into the machine, fill it with the hottest water possible to get them pliable, turn it off, and let them soak. The next day, I let the *hojas* spin, without agitating, and only then, fill it up with hot water to soak again. Result—soft *hojas* and soft hands!

Then it's the roaster ovens that can facilitate the cooking of the meat and chickens to a succulent finish; the food processor to chop it all up; the blender to puree your *chile poblanos*, and then when no one is watching, dump *la carne, el pollo y los chiles* into your *cazuelas de barro* to begin *La Tamalada*.

Now, pick your recipe, gather your favorite ingredients ahead of time, and maybe add a new experiment or invention of your own, and go to your local *molino* to buy the *masa*. Turn on the music, get the tissues ready, and gather together all your *comadres*, relatives, and friends, the essential Team of *Tamaleros* and begin.

You are now on your way to the best tamales of the year. But don't forget what my sister, Toni Solís from Ft. Worth, says: The tamales aren't good if the gossip isn't hot. So enjoy this little book with my own hints, *secretitos* and recipes. But don't forget to develop your own special family rituals and traditions to initiate your very own *Tamalada*.

RECIPES

Making the tamales- from 96 year old Tia Hope to Judge Guerrero to Vincent Valdez, artist, to Professor Olguin to the littlest hands.

Tamales de Puerco
Makes 6 dozen

Meat Filling

1. Cut the meat into large squares and put it into a large pot with the onion, garlic, salt, and peppercorns. Barely cover the meat with water and bring to a boil. Lower the flame and simmer the meat until it is tender—about an hour or so.

Set the meat aside to cool off in the broth. Strain the meat, reserving the broth, and chop meat roughly.

2. Cover chiles and comino seeds with water and bring to a boil. Let them stand until chiles are soft and water cools. When they are cool enough to handle, slit them open and remove the seeds and veins. Using a *molcajete* or a blender grind/blend them along with the comino into a paste.

Melt the lard, add the chile paste and sauté for about 3 minutes stirring all the time. Add the meat continuing to cook until the flavors meld. Add some of the broth and let the mixture cook for about 10 minutes over a medium flame. Filling should not be watery. Add salt as necessary.

Making the masa

1. If you get your *masa* from a *molino*, ask for *masa* for tamales or *masa quebradita*. If you use MASECA, get the one for tamales, which makes a very good *masa*, and follow the directions.

INGREDIENTS:

Meat Filling ✳ ✳ ✳
6 lbs	pork butt
1	onion
6	cloves garlic, peeled
3	tsp salt
6	peppercorns
Water to cover	
8	chile anchos (dry)
1 Tb	comino seeds

Masa ✳ ✳ ✳
6 lbs	masa from molino or
4 lbs	MASECA, follow directions
1 lb	lard
6 tsp	salt
1 tsp	baking soda
	broth

Shucks/hojas ✳ ✳ ✳
6 lbs	hojas/corn shucks
Hot water to cover.	

2. Melt the lard. Using a large mixer (Kitchen Aid) mix *masa*, salt, baking soda, broth, and adding lard a cup at a time. Continue beating for 10 minutes or so, until a 1/2 teaspoon of the *masa* floats in a cup of cold water (if it floats you can be sure the tamales will be tender and light). Beat until fluffy and semi-shiny. *Masa* should be of a stiff consistency but spreadable.

Preparing the hojas/corn shucks

1. *Hojas* are corn husks that are dry and papery but usually are clean of silks, trimmed and flattened ready for use when you buy a good brand. To soften them for use, pour plenty of very hot water over them and leave them to soak for several hours. If you have a top loader washing machine, clean the machine well using vinegar, rinse, and you can soak the *hojas*/shucks there. DO NOT agitate, but only use the spin cycle. You can soak them twice filling washer with hot water. Shake them well to get rid of excess water and pat them dry with a towel.

Making the tamales

2. Using a tablespoon or a knife, spread a thin coating of the *masa* over the broadest part of the shuck, allowing for turning down about 2 inches at the pointed top. Spread the dough about 3 inches wide and 3-1/2 inches long.

Spoon some filling down the middle of the dough (about 1 tablespoon. Fold the sides of the shucks together firmly. Fold up the empty 2 inch section of the *hoja*, forming a tightly closed "bottom" and leaving the top open).

Cooking the tamales

3. Fill the bottom of large soup pot or a tamale steamer with water up to the level indicated and bring to a boil.

Put either a *molcajete* or a bowl at the bottom of steamer and fill in with left over *hojas*. Stack the tamales upright, with the folded down part at the bottom. Pack firmly but not tightly. Cover the tamales with more corn shucks. Cover the top of the steamer with a dishcloth or thick cloth. Cover the steamer with a tightly fitting lid.

Cook tamales for about 2-1/2 to 3 hours over a medium flame. Keep water in a teapot simmering so that you can refill the steamer when necessary.

To test the tamales for doneness, remove one from the center, and one from the side of the steamer. Tamales are done when you open the *hoja*, the *masa* peels away easily from the *hojas*, and the tamal is completely smooth.

Filosofía de Tamales
¿Y un tamal es en teoría un tamal, como un taco es un taco? ¿No? El relleno es lo de menos, como sabemos de la preparación de los tamales fuera de Greater Mexico.
—Arturo Madrid, Ph.D.

Tamales de Pollo con Rajas

1. Boil the chicken in enough water to cover. Cook until done. Drain chicken, shred it, and save broth.

2. Boil tomatillos until soft and blend.

3. Flash fry the chile poblanos in hot oil. Cool and peel. Remove seeds and cut into silvers.

4. Heat the oil in a large deep olla or skillet over medium heat. Add onions and garlic, sauté. Stir in tomatillos and chicken, add chicken broth and cilantro. Season to taste. Cook over medium heat until liquid is reduced.

5. Follow the previous recipe for preparing the masa and hojas, making the tamales, and then cooking them.

INGREDIENTS:

Filling ✳ ✳ ✳

1 coarsely shredded cooked chicken and chicken broth

4 large chile poblanos fresh

3 tablespoons olive oil

2 garlic cloves, mashed

10 green tomatillos, water to cover

1 cup chopped cilantro

½ chopped onion

Salt

Ground black pepper to taste

Corn kernels can be added, either fresh or canned

The Havana Connection

Tamales in Cuba are just like the ones in Mexico City, according to Patricia Pratchett. There was even a popular cha-cha in Cuba in the 1950's called "los Tamalitos de Olga" by the Orquesta Aragón. Check it out on YouTube!

http://www.last.fm/music/Orquesta+Arag%C3%B3n/+videos/+1-X3vJ3FF-n7w

Tamales that won't upset the Rabbi or the Doctor

By Olga Garza Kauffman

Mexican cooks and their Latin American *co-madres* have always adapted the food they lovingly prepare for their families to fit the culture, ingredients, and needs of their surroundings. Especially true for the Latino Diaspora in *los Estados Unidos*, these adaptations have not always resulted in positive health outcomes. The modern use of hydrogenated oils such as Crisco, saturated animal fats, and highly processed flours have resulted in a severe health crisis among Mexican Americans. Latinos have the highest incidences of diabetes, stroke, and high blood pressure in this country. My mother, Reyna Garza, learned to adapt her kitchen repertoire in a flash when, after 40 years of making tamales from her mother's and grandmother's recipe, she had to cook healthy, low-fat meals for a husband with severe diabetes. She became a grandmother to two Jewish grandchildren who do not eat pork or mix milk and dairy. She quickly learned to make delicious meals and tamales without pork or lard, and became known for her delicious bean and cheese tamales. She now makes tasty chicken tamales that my Tía María sells out of her small kitchen in Harlingen, Texas. *Las comadres mexicanas* have always had a knack for innovation and adaptations, especially when it comes to their families' well-being. *¡Que no ni no!*

Tamales Dulces

INGREDIENTS:

Filling * * *

1 cup brown sugar or 1 piloncillo

1 cup water or orange juice

1 cup raisins

1 cup pecans, chopped

1 cinnamon stick

1 small can shredded coconut

1. Boil cinnamon stick in water/orange juice along with brown sugar or the piloncillo until dissolved.

2. Add raisins and pecans. Cook until liquid has reduced. Then add coconut. Mix sweet filling into enough masa to make tamales.

3. Follow the previous recipe for preparing the masa and hojas. Make these tamales a lot smaller. This time put about a tablespoon of the sweet masa into the center of the hoja. Tie the hoja together with a strip of the shuck, then steam.

Healthy Tamales

Healthy Masa ✳ ✳ ✳
1-1/3 cup (no trans-fat) vegetable oil or shortening such as Smart Balance or Spectrum

1-1/2 teaspoon salt

1-1/2 teaspoon baking powder

4 cups freshly ground masa for tamales

2 cups (approximately) low-salt chicken broth

"Arizona Rustic" Green Corn Tamales ✳ ✳ ✳
5 cups fresh white corn kernels

1 lb. low-fat mozzarella cheese

5 mild green chiles

½ cup canola oil

1 tsp. baking powder

1 tsp. salt

1 cup Stevia.

Roughly grind corn, add oil and dry ingredients. Masa will contain some whole kernels. Cook chiles on open fire, remove seeds, and cut in strips. Spread masa on shucks. Fill each with a strip of cheese and a strip of green chile, and steam till done.

Veggie Filling ✳ ✳ ✳
1 cup each of grated zucchini and carrots

1 cup each of frozen corn and black beans

1 onion, diced

2 Hatch chiles, seeded and chopped

¼ cup chopped cilantro

1 minced garlic clove

Cumin, salt, and pepper to taste

Olive oil

Bean and Cheese Filling ✳ ✳ ✳
5 cups beans refried in olive oil

Salt, chile, and garlic to taste

1 long strip of mozzarella cheese per tamal

Scientific Rationale Supports Healthy Recipe Tamales

Ninety-one percent of the cause of Type 2 diabetes is eating too much animal fat, too few vegetables, fruits and whole grains, and doing too little physical activity. The cure will come if we go back to our ancestral Native American lifestyles—eating more animal protein, vegetables, fruits, and whole grains, and being more active. With the Christmas holidays coming on, the healthiest tamales are those made of corn, vegetable oil, frijoles, and jalapeño. With these ingredients you have your healthy proteins (frijoles), healthy carbohydrates (corn and jalapeño) and healthy fats (vegetable oil).

—Roberto P. Treviño, M.D., Director, Social & Health Research Center

Go Gourmet
Sautee chopped shrimp and cilantro in olive oil and season with oregano for a unique filling.

✳ ✳ ✳ ✳ ✳ ✳ ✳

ELECTORAL TAMALES

❧ ⚬❁⚬ ❧

During the famous González-Goode cam-
paign for U.S. Representative, candidate
Goode used to "get the Mexican vote" by
rounding them up, taking them to a beer-
and-tamales rally, and then driving them to
the polls. Henry B. González answered with
a great slogan:

> *"Drink Goode's beer*
> *and eat Goode's tamales.*
> *But go to the polls*
> *and vote for González!"*

- Ernesto M. Bernal, Ph.D., educator

ELISA'S TAMALES

by Diana Doria and Chris Alderete

✳ ✳ ✳ ✳ ✳ ✳ ✳ ✳ ✳ ✳ ✳ ✳

My paternal grandmother was named Elisa Burciaga Rodríguez and she made the best tamales in all of San Antonio. She was a great cook, and working in the Robert B. Green Hospital kitchen for years gave her a lot of practice. Although everything and anything she made was delicious, she was best known for her tamales and her fruitcakes. In her latter years, she supported herself by making these favorites for many regular customers, among them Red Berry, Fred Seaman, Sol Casseb, Albert Peña, Henry B. González, and many of the city's power brokers. She was known as a "West Side Boss" and would guarantee so many votes for a candidate each election, for a fee, of course. This is how she came to know so many politicians and how they came to know her delicious tamales.

My grandmother would start making tamales early in November, sometimes in October, in order to fill all of her orders. She would charge the outrageous price, 50 years ago, of $2 or $3 a dozen.

Dr. Bambi Cárdenas, retired President, University of Texas Pan American

Many customers would order 10 to 20 dozen at a time for all of their holiday parties. Lots of tamales and lots of work!

My grandmother was a very strict, hardworking woman. There was no idle time for her or for those around her. My jobs during tamale-making season were to make sure the husks, in tubs all over the kitchen, were fully immersed in water, and then to *embarrar*, spread the masa on the husks. She had a very definite method of how this was to be done, in order to have the thin layer of *masa* that her tamales were known for. (To this day, I will not participate when family and friends make tamales—been there, done that.) Her most popular filling was chicken, but my favorite was her no-filling sweet tamales. She would add sugar, cinnamon and raisins to the leftover masa to make the most delicious, sweet tamales I have ever tasted … my reward for my hard work. Many family members, chefs, and customers, asked her for her tamale recipe, but she never ever gave it out. Her secret recipe for the best tamales in San Antonio died with her.

El Molinillo

Melony with Great-great-
grandmother Vasquez's *molinillo*

El Platón

Emily with Great-grandfather
Riojas' plate

Ya Ya's Girls
Talk Tamale

✶✶✶✶✶✶✶✶✶✶✶

"I like tamales because they are in between a taco and an enchilada."

—Melony, 7 years old

" Three good things about making tamales are:
1. Being with your family,
2. Having an excuse to get messy, and
3. Finally—eating the tamales!"

—Emily, 11 years old

"I remember making tamales when I was five and there being
so many women I didn't know, but who all seemed to know me.
They commented on how big I was, how beautiful I'd gotten, and
customary things people say when they haven't seen a kid for a
while. I remember mixing *masa* with my hands and trying to get
all the sticky *masa* off after I was done, which annoyed me! But I
still loved mixing masa. I always liked the chicken ones because I
thought that I was a big girl for eating the spicier one."

—Madeline, 14 years old

"When I was about 7, I walked into the kitchen to see my grandmother Ya Ya holding a pig's head in the kitchen sink and smash-
ing it with a hammer, in order to get to the meat on the inside... or
something to that effect. She remembers me screaming. It was not
what I was expecting!

—Erica, 21 years old

"When I think of tamale making, I see a kitchen filled with friends and family, laughing, and telling stories. The family spirits are there, too. My uncle David is standing by the table thrilling us with poems from his youth. My grandmothers are remembering the tasty tamales they made decades before I was born. My own children and nieces are in the kitchen now—squealing at the pig skull and lard, but happily eating the tamales anyway. My mother is there, everywhere, welcoming newcomers, grinding the chilies to season the meat, and spreading the gossip (I mean *masa*). The men are on the outskirts of the kitchen, taking in the aroma of this most familial of meals while they tend to their own fires outside on the grill. My sister, aunts, cousins, and I complete a circle around the old table. Before long, our hands remember the rhythm of the *masa* and meat and the steaming pots are filled."

—Jennifer

Erica with Great-grandmother Nana's *molcajete*

"The girl talk at the tamalada is sacred—this is where the youngest listen and watch how the moms, Ya Ya, and Great Tías interact and tell stories and learn to be confident young women. Though what I will never forget is the image of Ya Ya, my mom, standing on a stool over the simmering *carnes*, stirring with a face of determination—and a spoon about as long as she!"

—Judy

Judy and Jennifer are Ellen Riojas Clark's daughters. Erica, Madeline, Emily, and Melony are her granddaughters. They are to be commended for surviving the many years of *tamaladas* which brought in people from all over the world to their family home. Ellen Riojas Clark has always been known affectionately to her daughters and granddaughters as "Ya Ya".

Art by Juan Miguel Ramos, 2006.

Madeline with Nana's *palote*

The Tamale Tree

~ ❧ ~

Eloisa and Anita Tafolla, two young Mexican American college students in Indiana in the 1920s, wrote home to San Antonio that they were really missing their Mexican food, so Mamá sent older brother, Fidel L. Tafolla, for whom SAISD's Tafolla Middle School is now named, in the family Model T truck to take them homemade favorites, among them tamales. Their college dormmates had never seen or tasted anything like it, and soon everyone was invited to join in the feast. One girl, intrigued by the delicious delicacies, kept fingering the empty shucks on the plate until finally, she asked, "Exactly what kind of tree do these grow on?"

Tamales y Mas

by Robert Flynn

Whenever we went to Vernon, the county seat and 12 miles from my father's farm, I begged Mother and Dad to buy tamales to take home with us. A tall, slender, elderly African-American made tamales and stood on a street corner, selling them out of a steaming, red-and-white, two-tone, two-wheeled cart. Tamales were my favorite food, even more than my mother's fried chicken or fried steak with fried potatoes and fried bread.

Because my father grew corn, the tamale man sometimes came to the farm for shucks. When he did, he gave us tamales for the shucks. That was a special time, like Christmas morning without the presents but with the wonderful smell that promised tamales.

In the summertime I drove a tractor to make money for college. Since I was out in the country, I had to take a lunch with me. I told my mother I wanted tamales. Every morning before hand-cranking the tractor, I placed the tamales beside the manifold and by lunchtime the tamales were steaming. Mother asked me a couple of times if I wanted a change in diet! When I added catsup or picante sauce to the tamales, I had the food pyramid for lunch every day. Bread, meat, vegetables.

When I went to Baylor a gang of us discovered Charlie Lugo's, a wonderful Mexican restaurant where you could buy tamales by the dozen. They may have had half-orders as well but I wasn't a half-way kind of guy. I always ordered a dozen, and one night won a tamale-eating dare by using my dozen as an appetizer and then savoring those my comrades had abandoned on their plates.

About a year after our marriage, my wife, Jean, became ill with what was then called stomach flu. I told her to go to bed, I would run the kitchen. I opened a can of chili and a can of tamales and offered to share it with her. She said the stomach flu had ruined her appetite.

My wife and I lived in North Carolina a couple of years, a place so removed from reality that the grocery stores had never heard of tamales, not even Wolf Brand. When we returned to Texas for occasional visits, we loaded the car with tamales before returning to the third-world state.

When we moved to San Antonio, we found tamales, good tamales, but not the perfect tamales the tamale man made. Jean and a fellow-teacher, a friend I will call Celina Ríos Mullan, went on a quest to make the perfect tamale. And they did. Their tamales were so good their friends wanted some. Jean and Selena decided in the spare time they had from teaching, grading, after school parent counseling, bus-duty and hall-duty, they would make and sell tamales. Each agreed to take orders from others. At the end of the day, they had sold 174 dozen tamales. A whole hog's head worth.

Making and selling the tamales, boiling the shucks, cooking and plucking the meat from the hog's head, mixing in venison so they were not so fat, rolling out the tamales, wrapping them in shucks required more than twenty straight hours of work. It also left the kitchen, the sink, the stove, the meat grinder, the floor from the kitchen to the bathroom and to the back door a wreck. But they had also turned out some perfect tamales. One more weekend would fill the order if they didn't take any more orders.

More orders did come, and they expanded their enterprise into Christmas tamales and empanadas.

They talked of quitting teaching and going into the tamale business. Their husbands suggested names for the company. My contribution was Aw Shucks! Instead they chose Tamales y Mas. Celina's husband, G.E. Mullan, designed a logo. It was time to get out the calculator and see how many tamales they would have to make and sell to become competitive. If they didn't take into account the mess and the labor involved, their perfect tamales cost less than a dollar a dozen more than tamales they could buy from Ruben's or Willie Nelson's place in Helotes.

Jean declared that the calculator ruined their business and that she would no longer average my grades for me and instead would pay an accountant to prepare our income taxes. Today when I get hungry for tamales, she just says, "Call Ruben's."

"El que nace para tamal, hasta del cielo le caen las hojas"
- dicho mexicano sent in by David Cortez, owner, Mi Tierra Restaurant

MY FAVORITE TAMAL IS...

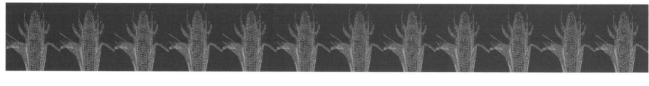

Roberto Treviño, M.D.
Social & Health Research Center
Los que hace mi mamá.

Rev. Eddie Bernal
St. Benedict Catholic Church
I hold it on deep religious conviction that the Virgen de Guadalupe made the BEST tamales.

María Antonieta Berriozábal
Former City Councilperson
The best ones are ALWAYS made by Wise Latina Women.

Rev. Virgilio Elizondo
Notre Dame University
The best tamales I ever ate were the ones prepared from the secret recipe inherited from the *cuñado* of the nephew of the mother-in-law of the daughter of Cuauhtemoc. BUT the funniest tamal I ever ate was in Monterrey when they served them with catsup and strawberry jelly.

Tamale Hint from Heloise #1

Once you love Mex-Tex, you can't leave home without it! When desperate, canned tamales are better than no tamales at all! Even ketchup works as *salsa*, if you're REALLY pining for your San Antonio home!

Vikki Carr
Grammy award-winning singer
When my husband Pedro told me that he would eat about 12 tamales *¡no lo podía creer!* In California we were lucky to finish 1 or 2 at the most! Little did I know that our tamales are much bigger than the ones my husband's family makes in San Antonio. I was born in El Paso, but raised in California, and tamales for us meant a big family gathering where everyone pitched in on Christmas Eve. There was so much laughter and of course, the *chismes of las comadres.* While the men put the *bote* on the fire outside to steam the tamales, we would go to midnight mass. When we returned, we had tamales *recién hechos, bien calientitos,* with hot Mexican chocolate or if we were especially lucky, we could have *café de la olla* with the adults, and that enabled us to stay up all night and feel so grownup. To me, tamales were always better 4 to 5 days later, sautéed in a skillet with *un huevo* on top— with the yellow of the egg flowing over the tamal and mixing with the beautiful red of the chile. MMMMMMMM!!!!!!!! Memories and visuals, what more could one ask?

Franco Mondini-Ruiz
Artist, Florence, Italy
I had a show in a gallery in über artworld cool Marfa, Texas. One of my pieces—a pile of dry, dusty tamale husks I had used as decor in my New York apartment. A Japanese collector just had to have it, so the tamale husks have found a new home in Tokyo.

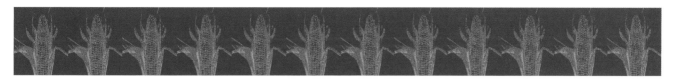

Antonia Castañeda, Ph.D.
Historian
My earliest memory of making tamales is going with my dad to the *matanza* in Toppenish, Washington, for a *cabeza de rez* and to the butcher for a *cabeza de puerco* for our Christmas tamales. To keep her children cleaning *hojas* and grinding corn, my mother would sing, *"Tamalitos, chiquititos; calientitos y sabrocitos!"* I can still savor those delicious and delicate tamales we cooked on an *estufa de leña* in my childhood.

María Eugenia Cossío-Ameduri
La Otra Abuela
The tamales I like most are from Yucatán, moist, *gorditos*, with lots of stuffing and very tasty. They are sensual; they appeal to our sight with the different colors, to our taste buds with all the seasonings, and to our ears with the crackling noise they make when unwrapped. I love the banana leaves that enfold the tamal like a gift, reminding me of noisy, theatrical, and edgy family dinners at my grandmother's house.

Rosa Catacalos
Director, Gemini Ink
Gathering quality goods is almost as fine as the actual making and eating. For years I've saved a string-bound package of *hojas* from Oaxaca, the shucks layered and fanned one-by-one into the shape of a very plump heart—and at the heart's point a tiny strip of paper slipped under the string—the bundle signed, "Ercilia."

Heloise
Syndicated columnist, Hints from Heloise
Mother and Daddy were stationed far from home in the 1950s, and going through serious Tamale Withdrawal Symptoms. So they had Patio Brand Tamales, 60 each in a gallon can, shipped to Arlington, Virginia, first, where my father was stationed at the Pentagon, and in later years (1958-62) to Hawaii where he was stationed at Hickham AFB.

They were not as good as the homemade ones you could get from the street carts in San Antonio during WWII, but they were very good. Daddy would take the legs out of the dining room table and side tables and make a long table to sit on the floor, sometimes adding plywood to make the table still longer. Mother would make a huge pot of chili and steam the tamales, then put coals in hibachi pots and lay the tinfoiled steamed tamales on them.

The "table" was covered with newspapers, and it was easy to just discard the corn husk on the table. Made for easy cleanup after. I think they got this from the way the Cajuns ate Mud Bugs. Most put the Chili over the tamales. There were also lots of Saltine Crackers, Fritos, Heinz Ketchup, and McIlhenneys Hot Sauce. Daddy would fill the bath tub with ice and beer, and about 12 to 20 people would sit on the floor and have a great time. Once, someone ate 30 or 40 tamales at one sitting. Mom and Dad were kinda famous for their Chili and Tamale Parties.

Cecilia Herrera
Diplomat, U.S. Embassy, Venezuela
I made my first tamale when I was 12 years old. My Aunt Frances invited a neighbor to come help us. I couldn't do anything right. The neighbor kept slapping my hand until I got just the right amount of *masa* on the shuck and just the right amount of chicken in the *tamal*. Thirty years later I found myself spending an entire day making tamales with family and friends to be enjoyed New Year's Eve. Forty-three years later, I find myself in Caracas, Venezuela, looking forward to the Venezuelan *tamal* called an hayacka, made with chicken, pork, beef, fruit, vegetables and plenty of *masa*. A rose by any other name smells as sweet, and that is how I feel about tamales. They are wonderful. And every reiteration is made with love and sacrifice for the family and friends that enjoy them.

Texas State Senator Leticia Van de Putte
The only thing better than making tamales "*con las mujeres de la familia,*" is eating them, "*sin los hombres en la cocina!*"

> ### Tamale Hint from Heloise #2
>
> **Need fast food and a tamale to go?**
> My father used to eat them like a push-up popsicle, standing over the sink, or with just a napkin. Try it, it works. You CAN eat a tamale on the go!!

"El Curro", Willie Champion
Flamenco guitarrist
My favorite tamal is *de venado*. My father would hunt the deer, and my mother would turn it into tamales. *Las tamaladas* were always a mystery to me, almost a gathering of *brujas*. I remember that boys and men were asked to leave the house and only the women would gather in one selected home. Boys would play at the other neighbors' homes, and the men sat and talked and had their *cervecitas*. When we got home the tamales would emanate an aroma that I can STILL smell, after so many years. Now I realize that the women had left their problems and dreams and hopes in those tamales.

Teresa Champion
Flamenco dancer
My favorite *tamal* is *de dulce, con coffee caliente, escuchando la guitarra de mi marido Curro—¡Olé!*
   The memories I have of *tamaladas* are of my mother gathering with women at our house or at the comadres' house where there seemed to be more talking, laughing, and crying than cooking, but somehow the tamales got made.

Judge JoAnn de Hoyos
I love tamales that have been blessed by Father Eddie because he promises me that he takes the fat and calories out so I can eat as many as possible!

Sylvia Romo, C.P.A.
Bexar County Tax Assessor

My Abuelita made the best tamales ever. She was diminutive, strong, independent—and also a perfectionist. When she died, my sister and I attempted to duplicate her tamales via "high tech." We purchased a mechanical tamale maker that had two cylinders, one for the masa and one for the meat.

The entire family was relying on us to have "Abuelita-like" tamales for our Christmas gathering. The meat and masa were prepared according to Abuelita's specifications, and the aroma of the tamale meat filled the kitchen. We stuffed the meat and masa into the cylinders and cranked away. To our horrible surprise, instead of getting nice and neat tamales, the meat spurted upward toward the ceiling and ended up on the walls, ceiling, floor, and everywhere you can imagine. The kitchen was a disaster area covered with a red splotchy substance. The following year, we decided to go the "old fashioned" way. Sometimes, tradition just shouldn't be replaced.

María Hernández Ferrier, Ph.D.
President, Texas A&M University, San Antonio:

My tamale story will probably be different than any other good Mexicana— my grandmother made horrible tamales! So one year we got together and told her that we didn't want her to work so hard so we would get them at Goas Tamale Factory. Goas was great and that became our family tradition—Goas Tamales every Christmas and New Year's.

> ### Poesía Infantil—Bedtime Versitos
> *"Tamalitos calientitos,*
> *días de fiesta, tan dulcitos."*
> —Pat Mora, award-winning children's author
> and poet, New Mexico

Diana Barrios Treviño
Owner, Los Barrios Restaurant

My first memory of my family's tamale-making career began when Belén, our nanny, drafted my brother, sister, and me into her tamale-making army. I was about nine years old and innocent—innocent of the amount of work that it entailed! About one month, two large bins of tamale shucks, and thousands of tamales later, we were ready to feed an army, the whole navy and possibly have a few left over to freeze for later.

Guillermo Nicolás
President, 3N Group

One of my favorite childhood memories was going to my *Welita's* house in Rosita, Coahuila, Mexico for New Year's Eve, sitting in her huge kitchen, and being served a plate of hot, beautiful, plump, sweet tamales, dressed in their shuck and tied with a perfect bow!"

Juan Mendieta
Miami Dade College, Florida

I love *tamales cubanos*. My favorite is *un tamal de jamón en su hoja, mojo de ajo*, pickles, pimento, lime, and crackers.

Henry de la Paz
Fashion designer
When I was little, my *niñera*, Torita, used to make me pink tamales made with coconut! They are still my favorite. But there's a woman back in Brownsville, Gloria Brooks, the Tamale Diva, who's my Grandma's best friend. Once I tasted her incredible tamales and asked, "How can I get some of THOSE? My Grandma looked at me with that *"No seas tonto"* look and said, "You have to get on a waiting list to get them!" Now THAT's a tamal!

Sandra Cisneros
Author
Fat tamales are my favorite; I mean the ones made in Central Mexico and shaped like Mexican feet. Not the little sardine-shaped ones folks eat in Northern Mexico and Texas.

Mary Alice Cisneros
San Antonio City Council
A *tamalada* is a special time when the seasoned tamal-maker teaches the inexperienced how to *embarrar* and keep keep the family recipe exactly as our *abuelitas* did in the past. Whether the occasion is Christmas or New Year's, tamales bring home the flavor of tradition.

The Honorable Julián Castro
Mayor, City of San Antonio
Chicken tamales with green chiles, and maybe some jalapeños in there for good measure.

Rosie Castro
Community activist and mother of the Mayor and State Representative
My favorite tamal is the *chile colorado con puerco* that were made at home when I was growing up in San Antonio's Westside. One day in El Paso, I was introduced to the most delicious green chile and cheese tamal I ever tasted. BUT, I would never say that El Paso had a better *tamal* then San Antonio! We are the *tamal* capitol of the universe.

Lisa Wong
Owner, Rosario's Restaurant
My sweetest tamale memory is the ritual that started at the molino... proceeded to the *carnicería*, and ended in Mom's warm kitchen. Her goal was to make everyone's favorite, so beef, chicken, and *frijoles* were each prepared to perfection. The final touch, though, was making our prized stash—the best sweet tamales in the world. These we would share over coffee every Sunday morning while they lasted. There was nothing like it. Sweet tamales, a little *cafecito*, my mom and me. This was her special time—her *hoja de cariño* for me and between us.

Elena Guajardo
Formerly City Council
On a study program in León, Guanajuato, I had tamales *de helote, fresas, dulces, y de maza con piñón* nuts. A wonderful tamalada experience. *Viva Tamales!!!*

Arturo Sandoval
Grammy award-winning Latin jazz musician, Miami, Florida
Mi tamal favorito es con carne de puerco.

Jesse Treviño
Artist and muralist
I'm a plain old-fashioned pork *cabeza tamal* eater. My mom and my sisters made the tamales. I just kept away until it was time to eat. I didn't get too involved in the making just the eating. And for me, it is pork tamales that are the only real tamales in San Antonio.

Bill Sinkin
**President, Solar San Antonio;
Chair, Hemisfair '68 Committee**
Years ago, I remember a sure-fire way we always knew it was Christmas time in San Antonio. One of the places we all had to go when Christmas rolled around was Centeno's on Commerce Street. They always had about a hundred hogs' heads propped up in a ring around the top of the building. You could talk tamales all you wanted, but when you saw that array of a hundred hogs' heads, then you KNEW it was time for tamales!

Texas State Representative Joaquín Castro
I love *los tamales de pollo*, with little bits of jalapeño sprinkled in.

Blanca Aldaco
Owner, Aldaco's Mexican Restaurant
My favorite *tamal* is the sweet corn tamal. Growing up in Guadalajara meant that close to dusk, the ladies who made tamales showed up either at the *"glorietas"* (roundabouts) or the plazas to sell their tamales. These freshly handmade tamales were simply delicious—light, fragrant, fluffy, and very tasty.

Felix Padrón
Office of Cultural Affairs, San Antonio
... Aaah... tamales, especialmente tamales cubanos hechos por mi abuela Estrella Santos. She's gone now, but her *tamales hechos para celebrar las pascuas y el fín de años eran de primera.* Sitting *en el patio de la casita en Pastorita*, making green bolsitas *de* corn husks and filling them with creamy corn was a work of art. Every once in a while *me encontraba con un trozo de puerco asado en su centro. ¡Qué rico eran esos famosos tamales cubanos!*

Ta-mal Economics
"When I was little I could tell if things for my family taban mal: a fat-jowled pig's head on the table ready for boiling meant we weren't having tamales de fifoles for Crismas."

—Juan Rodríguez

Edward James Olmos
Actor and director
"If they make a tamal that's vegetarian with fideo in it, I can PROMISE you that'll be my favorite!"

Dr. Joe J. Bernal
Former State Senator of Texas
Definitely the MACHO TAMAL! When in the "Tamal Assembly Line", you run out of meat—then you add *frijoles*. Until you run out of *frijoles*—then you add *pasas*. Then you have tamales *de pasas*—until you run out of *pasas*. Then you add sugar to the *masa*, to make 'em "sweet tamales." Then, when you run out of ALL the ingredients except the *masa* – you end up wrapping up the *masa* all by itself!!! That's a MACHO!!!

Cary Clack
Columnist
You know what the worst kind of tamales are? When there's not enough. I've heard that there are people who actually don't like tamales and I've heard of people who can only eat one or two tamales at a time. The reason tamales are sold by the dozen is so that I can make two meals of them—five hours apart. The first tamales that captured my heart, tummy and taste buds were sold at an East Side ice house on the corner of East Commerce and South Pine three blocks from my house. To this day just hearing the word "tamales" makes me...crave..them...so...very... very...much...oh God...gotta go.

A Villarreal-Russell Family Perspective

Texas State Representative Mike Villarreal:
When I was at Harvard, Mom would send me tamales grouped and wrapped in aluminum foil and boxed with dry ice. I enjoyed a reminder of my family and my home over each hot plate of tamales.

Jeanne Russell, Education Advisor to the Mayor: Tamales always remind me of Guatemala. The masa was thicker there, and they tasted smoky... after watching the women around the ovens, the smoke of the tamales rising into the clear air...

Bella Villarreal (age 5): Yum. But why do they put them in bamboo leaves?

Marcos Villarreal (age 4): (*chomp. chomp. bite. chew. smile. bite.*)

Naomi Shihab Nye
Poet
"As a vegetarian, it was often hard to find or trust the veggie ones... so, I never developed a relationship with them. I liked how cutely they were wrapped though!"

David Saldaña
The Krayolas
I was about 9 or 10, and I guess I had never seen how tamales were made. But I walked into the kitchen, and there was my Tía Saris and my Gramma 'Bualis up to their wrists in *GRASA*! They were smiling, their hands were glistening with grease, and it looked gruesome enough to traumatize me! I still eat'm, but that image will be etched in my memory FOREVER!

Terry A. Ybañez
Artist and teacher
Since I come from a family of tamale makers, I have several good memories, but the funniest is when I tried making tamales on my own. My mother gave me the recipe. I steamed my tamales and they smelled delicious, but when I tried one, it was as hard as a rock. I hadn't followed the part that said "Add a whole box of *manteca*, because I thought I'd be "healthier" with less. I had to throw my tamales into *el río de San Antonio* behind my apartment. I bet even the fish couldn't eat them.

Gregory G. Gomez
Lipan Mescalero Apache community advocate, Albuquerque, New Mexico
My all time favorite tamale story is how we, the Indigenous people of the Americas, gifted tamales to the world. My second all time favorite story—about the only bad tamale ever—the one I didn't eat...
Ayyyyyyyyy!!!

Rudolfo Anaya
Author
Pork and red chile tamales!

Ernesto M. Bernal, Ph.D.
Educational consultant
In the late 1940s my dad had a part-time job at an auto parts store. One fall, he took my Granny's pork tamales to work, and he shared some with his boss, who enjoyed them so much that by the early 1950s the man was a fixture at our Thanksgiving *Tamalada* and would eat—not kidding—a dozen by himself! But perhaps I remember his "packin' 'em down" best—he'd make a fist and then hammer down the top of his tummy. Granny's tamales were something else!

Arturo Madrid, Ph.D.
Murchison Distinguished Chair, Trinity University
Llegué tardíamente a ser aficionado y cognoscenti de tamales. El primer tamal que me captó me lo comí en La Flor de Lis en el DF, hace casi cuarenta años. La masa era blanca y airosa y el relleno de carne de puerco sabrosísimo... El segundo, lo preparó mi cuñada hace veinte años cuando cumplí 50 años. El relleno era de cangrejo. La masa estaba sufusa con el sabor del cangrejo, y sigo chupándome los dedos hasta el momento.

Andrew Weissmann
Award-winning chef
I LOVE the tamales of my wife's native Costa Rica, paired with an icy cold Imperial, but only after I determine what and where the meat comes from... (PURA VIDA!)

Celso Guzmán
Director of Workforce Diversity, ACCD
One great South Texas way to eat that culinary pre-Columbian time capsule, the humble yet enduring tamal, is to serve it up with another humble culinary accessory—ketchup. The sweet, slightly tangy, and vaguely salty, tomato-based sauce provides a vitalizing, palatable compliment to the ever adaptable tamal! Latently sweet, spiced-up masa, enfolding other tasty treats within... mmm.... Try it with a dash of salt—it's life changing!

Ricardo Romo, Ph.D.
President, University of Texas-San Antonio
My mother's recipe for *tamales de puerco* comes from HER mother, who got it from HER mother, who got it from HER mother and a long line of mothers before that. When my daughter was born in San Diego, my mother came by bus to meet her. Her bus was snowbound in El Paso for over 12 hours. When we finally picked her up at the bus station, her first concern was if the tamales arrived in good condition! Then her second concern was to meet her new granddaughter.

Margie Kilpatrick
Community advocate
As someone highly sensitive to sodium, where, oh where, can I get one without salt or salt substitute and no lard? A tamale salt-free, but prepared with lots of garlic and a healthy oil would allow me to once again savor this delicacy whose lack diminishes my and any San Antonian's Christmas celebration!

Tim Guillén
Co-owner, Timo's Coffeeshop
When I was 17, a Panamanian friend of mine invited me to her house for tamales. I THOUGHT I knew what we were going to eat! But when the plates were served, there was only one *tamal* on mine—and it was HUGE! You had to cut through the thick banana leaves, to find a tamal made of shrimp, rice, plantain, chicken, black olives, veggies, and who knows WHAT else! Tasted great.

Velma Villegas, Ph.D.
Superintendent of SWISD
My mom used to make my favorites, *de puerco*, with a pig's head. So, when I became a school principal, I decided to feed my *"gringo"* staff tamales for the Christmas social. Unfortunately, a tooth from the head was left in the meat and someone bit into it. Needless to say, I had some explaining to do about why tamales are best when you use meat from a pig's head.

Lionel Sosa
Marketing consultant
Tamale making was family time for us. My mom would make all kinds. Her favorite was refried bean tamales (olive oil, no lard) with lots of jalapeños. Chicken was next on her menu and finally, fat, square, sweet cinnamon tamales. She would never make pork tamales because she thought they weren't healthy enough. Mom was a health nut even back in the 40's and 50's. Now all my daughters and my gringa wife Kathy carry on the tradition—family and tamales at Christmastime!

Martha Medrano, M.D., MPH
Psychiatrist, UTHSCSA
My husband and I are from El Paso and the New Mexico area. When we first moved to San Antonio and ordered some tamales, we were shocked because they were so small, really tiny. We were under the impression that everything was bigger in Texas, especially in the heart of Texas (San Antonio.) Even after 30 years in SA, we still marvel at the tiny tamales and yearn for the big, fat, New-Mexico-style tamales.

Ana "Chá" Guzman, Ph.D.
President, Palo Alto College
Only those who hold *tamaladas* to be a sacred family tradition could believe that the amount of work is worth it! So most years I buy my tamales. However, one of the few years we decided to make them, someone showed up so scantily clad we threatened to put an *hoja* over her cleavage!

Norma Cantú, Ph.D.
Professor, University of Texas-San Antonio
Tamales have gone from Christmas food to anytime food, but for me they will always signify family at Christmas time. The *tamalada* remains a mainstay for my 7 sisters and I as we gather to celebrate the holidays at my mother's in Laredo. We make small, thin tamales the size of a fat ball point pen, stuffed with my mother's special recipe—passed down from mother to daughter for at least 6 generations—that includes raisins in the *guisado de puerco*. We also make chicken and refried bean tamales, and usually, *de azucar*—sweet tamales with raisins kneaded into the sweet dough and no stuffing.

Alicia Mena
Playwright and actor, *Las Nuevas Tamaleras*
How was I to know that a simple story about the humble tamal would bring so much joy to me and the many who have come to share the fun of *Las Nuevas Tamaleras*.

Aloha Tamales
When 15-year-old Celina Canales (now Price) won a cheerleading competition and an offer to go to a National Presentation at the Hula Bowl in Hawaii, her grandmother Margarita C. Hinojosa was determined to help her get there. She made and sold 300 dozen tamales, and her granddaughter jumped on a plane, still smelling the 3,600 tamales of love! ¡Que amor!

Las Divas

Sylvia Rodríguez:
Sweet! And this year I have created a new *tamal dulce. M'ija* named it "Sylvia's Delightful Desert Tamales"!

Mary Alice Cisneros:
My favorites are chicken and/or beans.

Alejandra I. Villarreal:
Chicken from Karam's on Zarzamora. Oh right, they're no longer there. Boo hoo!!!

Choco G. Meza:
De puerco con jalapeños.

Lupe Ochoa:
Pork tamales are my favorite, of course, but I have tasted some with cheese that were awesome.

Mary Esther Bernal:
¡Los tamales favoritos de las Divas—los que hace la Diva Sylvia !!!

Diana Doria and Chris Alderete:
Grandmother Elisa's sweet tamales.

Ellen Riojas Clark:
De pollo con rajas.

Franco Mondini-Ruiz
Artist, Florence, Italy
"One of the nicest compliments I ever got in New York City— asked by a fancy art client where I like to eat Mexican food in NYC, I hesitated, knowing how many New Yorkers resented the Puebla-cization of NYC. Then I fessed up, half-way expecting her to roll her eyes in dismay: "I love to buy the tamales from the street vendor ladies... from Puebla." She then gently responded that with its growing Mexican population, New York had become a kinder and more polite city."

María Antonieta Berriozábal
Formerly San Antonio City Council
Tamales is... *mi Mamá.* Tamales is... *mi Papá.* Papá, young and strong, would go to the *molino* at the corner of Cecilia and Picoso and buy "*un poquito de masa.*" Mamá would add the lard and salt, then *amasar* with her sturdy arms. She would cook the meat with all kinds of wonderful smelling spices and start *embarrando.* We kids got a place at the table to spread that *masa* but none of us quite mastered it. The most wonderful memory is the taste of that first big, hot, tamal to eat in front of Mamá. As years passed, Papá still got the *masa* but much less. He also had to *amasar* because Mamá's arms could not do it anymore. The lard became Crisco, and *puerco* became beef. Mamá contracted diabetes. Then one Christmas, there were no more trips to the *molino* by Papá and no more tamales from Mamá. Yes, tamales, is Mamá y Papá, together. Tamales is love.

Ernest Teneyuca
Emma Tenayuca's brother
My wife Irene made the best. I would make the masa and help her spread, and we'd make enough to feed all our employees for a month —which was her and I.

Sharyll Teneyuca
Attorney and Emma Tenayuca's niece
Once Uncle Ernest brought 40 dozen of Aunt Irene's homemade tamales, packed in dry ice, on the plane with him to visit us in Buffalo, New York. All our friends were completely smitten. We had to ration them like bars of gold. My son, Greg tasted one and said, "This is the best tamale I've had in my whole life." He was two years old at the time.

Sheriff Roland Tafolla
Bexar County, Texas
I was maybe 8 when one Christmas, my maternal grandmother, who lived with us, decided to make tamales. I remember my favorite of all the kinds she made was one called *tamales borrachos. The tamal estaba revuelto con masa y carne de puerco.* And the *carne* was not in the middle as usual. She told me that whatever *masa* and *carne* was left, they would just mix all together and by that time the men in the family would come in to help mix them late at night. The name, I think, comes from the fact the tamal itself is all disoriented and the men that (who had had a few by then) were also disoriented. *Medios borrachos—como los tamales o como los hombres de la casa.*

Juan Tejeda
Conjunto Atzlán and Coordinator,
Tejano Conjunto Festival
¡De frijol! Con rajas de jalapeño, with beer, and to the sound of *conjunto music. ¡Ajúaaa!*

Paul Bonin-Rodríguez, Ph.D.
Writer and performer
In December 2002, Michael Martínez and I convened a group of gay men aged 20 to 60 associated with ALLGO to make art. We called the project "*Compañeros.*" Our first order of business—*una tamalada, por supuesto.* Mind you, not one of us had ever led a *tamalada.* We had always been helpers, spreading the *masa,* rolling the tamales, or pouring more chocolate for the *compañeras* in the kitchen, but after a little time and a lot of tequila, we figured it out. And they were the best I ever ate (from what I can remember)!

Patty Ortiz
Executive Director, Guadalupe Cultural Arts Center
On one of my family's annual holiday *tamaladas,* as my sisters and I were first learning this tradition, we asked my dad what he was doing as he was *embarrando* the *masa* on the corn husks. He answered with humor and a twist of words, "I'm embarrassing the tamales!" To this day every holiday we make the tamales feel as self-conscious and uneasy as we can! I personally like the tamales that are lightly embarrassed more than the heavily embarrassed ones!

Graciela Cigarroa, **attorney, and**
Francisco Cigarroa, M.D., **Chancellor, UT System**
Nuestro tamal favorito es la caserola de tamal indio que nos preparaba nuestra abuelita Mane cada año nuevo.

Rebecca Almazán
Visual artist
Rules from my Mamá: "You cannot *embarrar las hojas* until you master washing and draining them. I will be the one to decide when and if you are worthy to graduate to *embarradora*. I will fill them, roll them, and only I will stack them in the *bote*."

My eldest sister Esperanza was her taster, as well as my brother Pedro. Shortly before she died in 1983, Esperanza and I took over as *tamaleras*, Mama tasted all the fillings: *carne*, chicken, beans, beans and cheese, and cheese and jalapenos. When the first tamales were done, we gave her the tamal to taste, and she said, with tears in her eyes, *"Ya no me necesitan—ustedes ya son las tamaleras."*

She died before the next *tamalada*. Esperanza took over, I continued to come to San Antonio during Christmas to help her. We laugh a lot now when we think of Mama as we tackle sixty pounds of masa for Christmas Eve. Some time ago, I bought restaurant aprons. I hand painted them with flowers, and hand lettered *HIJA DE TAMALERA*. Now I cannot schedule going back to Maryland to be with our daughters for the holidays until my sister gives me the new *tamalada* dates for a non-stop three day marathon. I am now the official taster!

Bryce Milligan
Writer, folksinger and publisher
With my guitar strapped to my motorcycle, making it to a gig in Gallup, New Mexico, in 1973, I stopped at a food stand all by itself in the middle of nowhere. A tiny *viejita* served up an enormous blue corn and green chile tamal that I can still taste. *Pero*, the tamales I love the best are the ones Mary and I make every year for the party we have after caroling and singing *Las Posadas*. You put the love in, you get the love back!

Tamalito Frito
No, I don't live in a Taj Mahal,
but I do have a tamal
warming up on my trusty *comal*.
¡Qué tal!
- Jacinto Jesús Cardona, poet

Tamal Grammar

❧ ⚬ ☙

WARNING:
If speaking Spanish, this is a grammar lesson;
if speaking English, this is a math lesson.
If suffering from an extreme case of Math Anxiety,
take two tamales, and enjoy: the lesson will engrave
itself on your psyche at the intuitive-gustatory level.

Wonder why so many waiters at restaurants cringe when you order "One tamale, please"? It's not because they find it impossible to believe anyone could eat just one. It's because the word "tamale" doesn't exist in Spanish. "Tamales" is the plural, and "tamal" is the singular. Yes, language and dialect (even mistakes) are contagious, and many Spanish-speakers have succumbed to the English habit of saying "a Tamale" in order to be understood. But to be impressively suave, if you're ordering just one "tamal" —drop the "e" (or at least smile, and be San Antonio-friendly- that works too!)

GEOGRAFÍA DE TAMALES

****

Siempre se hacen los tamales con dos ingrediente básicos—colaboración y optimismo. Y siempre se vuelve en hojas! Lo del relleno y las diferentes recetas refleja las circunstancias, los orígenes, y la geografía de la familia.

Mi Mamá, Veracruzana, hacía por tradición, tamales de carne de puerco en hoja de plátano—deliciosos, estilo Veracruz y tropical, que llevan jitomate en su guisado, y no son picosos.

En cambio en Oaxaca los hacen con carne de puerco también pero con mole negro muy sabroso.

Para el Día de Muertos, mamá hacía tamales de calabaza amarilla (de esa que hacen el pay tan rico en San Antonio), guisado con camarones y chilito rojo que no picara mucho. A veces tomaba ordenes para tamales de piña y fresa.

Pero el que me parece más ingenioso y original es originario de Pánuco, Veracruz: mide hasta un metro de largo y se llama ZACAHUIL. Lo hacen de masa de maíz no bien molido, que quede un poco quebrado y ya; ponen enuna mesa hojas de planta de plátano, y sobre ella extienden la masa; le colocan lo que lleva de relleno (carne de cerdo, res o pollo,cruda, revuelta con chile ya guisado; lo envuelven bien, y lo ponen acocer en un horno de barro que hacen en el suelo. Por otro lado ya tienen brasas hechas de leña, y una vez que lo cubren con hojas, lo tapan con brasas y tierra. Y queda muy sabroso. Los hacen para banquetes y para vender en trozos, como quiera la gente.

Sabrosísimo!

En Tamaulipas preparan tamal que llaman "gorda de acero". Revuelven masa preparada con manteca y sal, le echan carne o pollo guisado, la colocan en un molde y lo meten al horno.

Los tamales "norteños" y los de Tejas son muy pequeños. Los de Zacatecas llevan carne o pollo con chile guisado y van en hoja de maíz, y antes de meterlos a cocer en una olla, los riegan con más caldillo del mismo chile guisado. A veces le ponen una pierna entera de pollo en cada tamal o un pedazo grande de carne. También hay tamales "locos" que son los que hacen sólo con sal y manteca , y envueltos en hoja de maíz.

Los tamales de Chiapas llamados "padecitos", son de masa dulce y rellenos de una preparación de maicena con leche y azúcar.

Tamales Chiapanecos van en hoja de plátano, la masa con sal, rellenos de carne guisada, aceitunas y una ciruela pasa grande.

Y mis sobrinos me platicaron de los tamales de elote verde de Arizona, que tienen pedacitos de elote "blanco" fresco en su masa y contienen por relleno queso blanco con rajas de un chile verde que no pica. Ademas una señora en Flagstaff los hacía para su esposo según su dieta de bajar colesterol, y usaba aceite de canola y queso mozarella de bajo grasa. ¡Y su colesterol quedó mejor que nunca!

—Profesora Celina Marroquín de Hernández, 2009, México, D.F.

THE GEOGRAPHY OF TAMALES

****

Tamales are always made with two basic ingredients—collaboration and optimism. And they're always wrapped in leaves or shucks. The fillings and the different recipes reflect the circumstances, the origins, and the geography of the family.

My mother, a native of Vera Cruz, traditionally made pork tamales in banana leaves–a delicious Veracruz style and tropical, with tomatoes in the stew, and not very spicy.

In contrast, the Oaxaca region makes the pork tamales with a savory dark *mole*.

For the Day of the Dead, my mother made pumpkin tamales (like the delicious pumpkin pies of San Antonio) with a filling of shrimp and mild red chile pepper. Sometimes she took orders for tamales made with pineapple and strawberries.

But the one tamal I consider most ingenious and original is from Pánuco, Veracruz. It measures about three feet in length and is called a *ZACAHUIL*. It's made with a roughly ground corn *masa* that still has cracked pieces of maize in it, and is spread over a banana leaf. Over the *masa*, they place a filling of raw pork, beef or chicken mixed with chile. The banana leaf is wrapped around it well and it's cooked in a clay oven built into the ground with coals on one side. They place the tamales in the clay oven, cover it with more banana leaves, hot coals, and dirt. And the *zacahuil* comes out delicious! It is served at banquets or sold by the piece, according to ones' preference.

Beyond delicious!

In Tamaulipas they make tamales called "*gorda de acero*" or fat steel. They mix the dough with lard and salt, add a filling of meat or chicken, form into a mold pan, and cook in the oven.

Tamales Norteños from northern Mexico and those from Texas are very small. Those from Zacatecas are filled with meat or chicken, cooked with chile and put into corn shucks; before cooking, they are saturated with the same chile broth. Sometimes they put a whole chicken leg or a big chunk of meat into the tamal. "Crazy tamales" are made with just salt and lard and wrapped into corn shucks.

The tamales from Chiapas, called *padecitos*, are made with a sweet dough and filled with a pudding made of cornstarch, milk, and sugar. *Tamales Chiapanecos* are wrapped in a banana leaf, have a salty dough and are filled with sautéed meat, olives, and a large prune.

My nephews told me about green corn tamales from Arizona, which have kernels of fresh white corn in the masa and are filled with white cheese and a slice of mild green chile. A lady from Flagstaff even makes them for her husband who is on a strict low-cholesterol diet; she uses canola oil and low-fat mozzarella cheese, and his cholesterol level is lower than ever!

–Professor Celina Marroquín de Hernández, México, D.F., 2009

Translated by Ellen R. Clark

ANY tamales eaten on Christmas morning make one extra holy, but my FAVORITE ones are stuffed with meat and have to be eaten with COLD, cold milk! (I'm not kidding!)

- Posted by Rev. Eddie Bernal

....

How terribly un-kosher...

- Posted by Rabbi X

....

My father, son of a *Mexicana* from Monterrey, (from whence all of Mexico's Sephardic *judíos* hail) always said that anyone who would drink milk and tamales together was part of a gringo plot to malign Mexican-American cultural credibility. He always had HIS tamales with coffee.

- Posted by Carmen Tafolla

....

I disagree. The problem lies in Clary Clack. Clack's coverage of tamales in his columns is a clear case of a Methodist plot to undermine Baptist Cultural Creativity.

- Posted by Robert Flynn

....

Bob Flynn is part of a Baptist plot to destroy Methodists, tamales, and the culture of San Antonio as we now know it.

- Posted by Cary Clack

....

I, personally, think they're BOTH harboring terrorists. You can tell it by how they dress. Muslim law demands that all tamales be *halal* and be eaten with no alcohol at the table. They are especially tasty with *fesenjan mole*.

- Posted by Rashin Mazaheri

....

Let's keep the peace, folks. These kinds of discussions should be non-partisan, because everyone can understand the universal appeal of tamales, especially my dear Methodist brethren. Nothing quite as heartwarming as a Methodist Church Tamale Supper.

- Posted by Cary Clack

....

Discussing tamales with a Methodist is like discussing ham with a Rabbi. Gary Clack, Methodists have fewer recipes for tamales than Catholics have for communion wafers. Tamales with milk is not only repulsive to anyone who keeps kosher; it's offensive to anyone who loves tamales. Tamales can be appreciated only when taken with beer, dark beer like Guinness although Negra Modelo is an acceptable substitute. Methodists drink light beer with tuna fish casserole tamales.

- Posted by Robert Flynn

....

That reference to Negra Modelo... why do we have to bring race into this? Will it never end? Can't we all get along? I do, however, agree with my Sullen Baptist brother that milk with tamales is repulsive. You gotta have it with Big Red, the national drink of San Antonio.

One thing I will add about Methodists and tamales, as opposed to Baptists. Because our services are only 90 minutes long, we get home sooner to eat our tamales. We're on the third dozen by the time the Baptists wake up (three hours into their service) for the preacher's sermon.

- Posted by Cary Clack

....

Jerry Clack! That is one cheesy enchilada you are hurling at Baptists. Methodists think *tostadas* are overcooked flapjacks. Methodists think *nachos* are what *pistoleros* carve in the butt of their sixguns. Methodists believe *Gorditas* was killed by David with two smooth stones and five fishes. Methodists believe *Fajitas* was a Greek city visited by the Apostle Paul. Methodists believe that *Chalupas* was a camel ridden by one of the Wise Men who were guided by a star to the place where Jesus was born. Methodists search tortillas to find the face of John Wesley... Baptists believe in the Father, the Son, and the Holy King James Bible. And to paraphrase the Holy King James Bible, "By their tamales you shall know them." In the words of the immortal Tom DeLay, I have not yet begun to defame.

- Posted by Robert Flynn

My favorite tamales *son los que hace mi suegra*—and she's not even Jewish! (Much less Baptist or Methodist!)

- Posted by Al Kauffman

Amen.

- Posted by Cary Clack

I give up.

- Posted by Robert Flynn

No, I give up!

- Posted by Cary Clack

No, Cary, you are too kind and Methodists are too gentle to battle with fire-breathing, eyeball-rolling, take-no-prisoners Baptists.

You won, Cary, you're the better man, even if you are a—expletive deleted—Methodist.

- Posted by Robert Flynn

You're BOTH very kind, (for a Baptist and a Methodist) but I think I have the last word— Go in peace. And if you're thinking about eating MY plate of tamales, go FAR AWAY, in peace or not!

- Posted by Rev. Eddie Bernal

Anyone who messes with someone else's tamales, Father, would surely get arrested for Grand Theft Tamal.

- Posted by Chief Deputy Roland Tafolla

Anyone arrested for the basic human right of eating tamales deserves a good Civil Rights lawyer! And I'll take the case, but first—where did that recipe for kosher tamales go?
- Posted by Al Kauffman

You guys got it ALL wrong! The best tamales are the ones my mother used to make. And the only drink one should have with a nice hot plate of tamales—is a big, glass bottle of Coca-Cola. Not just any Coke, but a REAL Coke, the kind from Mexico, with real sugar.
- Posted by Susana Narvaez-Godinez

We hereby grant this book —every hoja of it—our Seal of Approval, as long as we can censor the words "Coke" and "Sugar" out. Otherwise, WE may need the kosher recipe PLUS a good civil rights lawyer!
- Posted by FDA (Frijoles Doctors Association)

As a member of the Southwest General Conference of the Latino Methodist Mafia y La Mera Mera Gran Tamalera, I have the last word. If Santa Claus can eat his tamales cold, I can eat mine with champagne. And that is the Grand Tamal Manifesto: cold tamales with cold bubbly!
- Posted by Ellen Riojas Clark

Bloggers:
Rev. Eddie Bernal, Pastor, St. Benedict Catholic Church
Cary Clack, San Antonio Express News columnist and author
Ellen Riojas Clark, Ph.D., Professor, University of Texas at San Antonio
Robert Flynn, Professor Emeritus and author, Trinity University
Al Kauffman, Attorney and Assistant Professor, St. Mary's University, School of Law
Rashin Mazaheri, Attorney and Owner, Shiraz Restaurant
Susana Narvaez-Godinez, Director of Endowment Administration, UTHSCSA
Carmen Tafolla, Ph.D., Author and Faculty, University of Texas at San Antonio:
Chief Deputy Roland R. Tafolla, Bexar County Sheriff's Office
Rabbi X

SHUCKS, MR. PRESIDENT

U.S. President Gerald Ford's visit to San
Antonio in 1975 is probably best remem-
bered for its well-publicized culinary faux
pas. When offered some of San Antonio's
best tamales, the president very politely
picked one up and bit in – shuck and all!
He was gently corrected by his San Antonio
host—and never made the same mistake
again. Eating a tamal with the shuck ON?
Hmmm.

—Mary Esther Bernal, bilingual educator and
former San Antonio ISD Board Member

A DELICIOUS HISTORY

✳ ✳ ✳ ✳ ✳ ✳ ✳ ✳ ✳ ✳ ✳ ✳ ✳

Once upon a *tamal*, on the lush, green continent of the Americas, a mother taught her daughter how to make tamales. Then THAT daughter taught HER daughter, and THAT daughter taught HER daughter, and soon, grandmothers and mothers, *tías* and *comadres* were teaching their *hijos* and *nietos* how to make the very tasty, fresh-steamed recipe. But good as each *tamal* tasted, each woman added her own touch, and an awful lot of love. And tamales became known in the Americas as the food of choice for special celebrations.

Valerie González, CEO, Delicious Tamales

Then one day, about 7,000 years later, the daughter of the daughter of one of these mothers, was sitting in a warm family kitchen, amid the *chisme* and the laughter, while her half dozen siblings and her *tías* and *abuelita* all worked together, following with extra love the special recipe handed down so long ago. She felt a deep *respeto* and pride in the cultural *herencia* that she was witnessing.

"¡Apúrate, Valerie! ¿Porqué paraste de embarrar? You're holding up the line!" her sister called.

But Valerie González was a dreamer, and she dreamed of someday passing on these *sabores* and this *cariño* to the rest of the world. Her father's words had impressed themselves on all seven siblings. "Educate yourself so you can better yourself." And so she and every one of her siblings went off to college at the University of Texas Austin, and got their degrees. Committed to helping her community, Valerie was involved in the social activism and Chicano politics of the late 70s, and then came to San Antonio to work on a Masters in Social Work at Our Lady of the Lake University. In 1980, Valerie and her then-husband invested $500 to open Delicious Tamales at 1901 Cincinnati St. In 1983, they opened a second location at 1330 Culebra Rd.

Today, Delicious Tamales is the leading manufacturer of tamales in San Antonio, selling more than 2.1 million tamales each year. That's 70 dozen tamales every 2 minutes! A woman-led corporation, Delicious Tamales was voted Best Tamales for ten consecutive years (1996-2006) in the San Antonio Express News Readers' Choice Awards, and listed as one of the top 25 Hispanic Owned Businesses in San Antonio by San Antonio Business Journal. With six locations, and open seven days a week, the 30,000 sq. ft. corporate headquarters on Culebra Rd. ships tamales, tamale cans, t-shirts, (and this book too!) to every state in the U.S. They make Pork, and Jalapeño Pork, Bean and Jalapeño Bean, Chicken and Jalapeño Chicken, Jalapeño Cheese, and sweet tamales of coconut, raisin and pecan. Each tamal follows the generations-old recipe, with stone-ground corn and fresh ingredients hand wrapped in corn shucks. Valerie Gonzalez, as President and CEO, works side by side with her daughters, Herlinda López and Iliana López, just like the very first mother-and-daughter tamales team did 7,000 years ago. And people anywhere in the U.S. hungry for a good tamal just dial 1-800-TAMALE-1 or go online at www.delicioustamales.com and their comadre Valerie will ship them the sabor of tradition, of women's collaboration, and of love.

But running a successful business doesn't mean that Valerie's community activism has stopped. On the Board of Directors of Madonna Center and active in many community-oriented projects, Valerie was approached with the idea of publishing this book as a fundraiser to benefit the Guadalupe Cultural Arts Center, and the artists of this Latino-Mexicano community. She generously agreed to sponsor the production of this edition. What a DELICIOUS tradition of *cariño*, collaboration, and *comunidad!*

Chaos Theory Tamales and Going Green

The best tamales I ever ate were some I only tasted one day in my whole life— and I can STILL taste them! They absolutely spoiled me. Two of my *tías*, while raising their kids, economizing on a budget, living far from a *molino*, and still doing the many chores related to living on a *rancho*, had invented an emergency recipe for tamales that didn't require *embarrando*, buying *hojas* and *masa*, or having the right quantities of ingredients. They grabbed the green *hojas* off "roast-enears" of corn, threw some *masa, cebollita, ajo, carne*, and fresh kernels of corn in a *sartén*, and then quickly scooped the cooked filling inside the green *hojas*, and steamed them. By supper, the best aroma filled the house. It became a family favorite, and I lucked out one afternoon when they were reminiscing about their "*tamales de helote*" and cooked up a batch. I can taste them to this day. I tried to duplicate it, but... ¡*ni pa qué decir!*

—Carmen Tafolla

CONTRABANDO Y TAMALES

—to the tune of "Contrabando y Traición" (La Camelia)
Lyrics by Carmen Tafolla, 1977, for the first of seven annual Tafolla & Co.
"Multi-Media Tamaladas." Sung and arranged by Juan Tejeda, 2008.

* * * * * * * * * * * *

Salieron de San Antonio.
Proceden desde Laredo.
Traían la petaca llena
De masa para tamales.
Eran Felipe el Relleno
Y Pilar la Tamalera.

Iban sentados tres puercos
En el asiento de atrás
Y un montonote de hojas
Entre Felipe y Pilar.
Y ella traía en su regazo
Diez galones de agua con cal.

Coro:
A una puerta llegaron,
La casa de una comadre.
Desempacaron las cosas
Y Pilar se puso a su jale.
Nunca se vió en el mundo
Tamalera mas picante.

Diez mil cada hora salían
Mientras Felipe empacaba.
El Cheby ya bien pesadito,
Y el Felipe ya bien cansado.
Al fin se sentó un ratito
A llenarse el buche 'e tamales.

De pronto se oyó una sirena;
Tres carros la casa enrodaron.
Ya les iban a arestar
La policia del estado
Por cruzar sin licencia la carne
Por la linea del condado.

Coro:
Pilar le dijo al Felipe,
"Yo no me doy por vencida.
Yo sí me se defender
De esta chifla'a policía.
Escóndate tú los tamales
Mientras yo les eche chispas."

Pilar calentó bien el orno
Y abrieron franca la puerta.
Un chile tiró a'i adentro
Con una mano de experta.
Saltó el jalapeño volando
Derechito como un balazo.

El aire, lleno de fuego,
Y ya se oían explotar
A todos lados las bombas,
Los jalapeños de Pilar.
La policía no aguantaba
El fuego y el llorar.

Coro:
Pilar le dice a su comadre,
"Ya casi se han aguitado.
Y creo que los tamales,
Felipe los haya ocultado."
Pero a ese momento
Se oyó un terrible truenazo.

Por tragarse los tamales
Felipe se reventaba,
Pero borró la evidencia
Y ya no hallaron nada.
La policía solo halló
Una hojita tirada.

The original El Popo Tortilla Factory; Roberto Borrego, Jr., far left.
Photos courtesy of Roberto Borrego Jr.

THE FAMILY BUSINESS

✳ ✳ ✳ ✳ ✳ ✳ ✳ ✳ ✳ ✳ ✳ ✳

It's a lesson in history. About tortillas, about tamales, about cultura, about our town. He drops names belonging to old San Antonio families that lived here a century ago, sprinkles in tidbits of their encounters with El Popo Tortillería and Adelita's Tamales. He remembers Henry B. Gonzalez, the first Mexican American US Congressman, as #90 at Blessed Sacrament, and Charles Becker, then-owner of Handy-Andy grocery stores, in the moment he was convinced by José Oliveras, the first Mexican American on the San Antonio City Council, to put El Popo tortillas in his supermarkets. On the first day, they sold hundreds of tortillas and their business took off like never before. "The other big grocery store wouldn't even give us the time of day... wouldn't even hear of putting tortillas on their shelf! In 1949," Señor Roberto Borrego, 79, shakes his head, "white business men didn't see tortillas as something with any business potential." Today, according to the Manta website, Adelita's makes between 10 and 20 million dollars yearly.

Señor Borrego keeps a picture of his grandfather on the old fashioned adding machine in his office. Borrego praises his entrepreneurial skills and the

Roberto Borrego, Jr., owner.

way he always dressed to the nines with a coat and tie. His father, Roberto Borrego Sr., founder of the El Popo Tortilla Factory, began his business career in 1925 as a salesman for La Vencedora Tortilla Factory, who later became his competition. "I remember going with Papi to Mi Tierra Restaurant to have coffee early in the day, when the La Vencedora staff would also come drink coffee. Papi would make good use of that time to find out what the competition was up to." Borrego, Sr. introduced the selling of tortillas outside the tortilleria, starting first with "house to house" sales and from there into grocery store sales. In 1930, Roberto married Beatrice Martinez and in 1938 they rented a corner property at Houston and Leona Streets in San Antonio, where they founded El Popo Tortilla Factory.

They started with a *nixtamal molino*, a *metate*, and a hand-cranked corn tortilla press. The couple worked long hours to grow their business. They had three sons, Roberto, Jr., Raul, and Richard. In 1945 he was the first business in San Antonio to purchase tortilla machinery—a tortilla oven from California—which was new and revolutionary equipment in the tortilla industry.

El Popo expanded to a larger site in 1955 at Ruiz and Brazos, and it is here that his sons developed their business into the most modern and productive plant in its time in the South Texas area. During these years, Roberto Borrego was active in designing a pneumatic press to make flour tortillas. He was the first to install a horizontal paper wrapping machine. Later he purchased a machine to hermeticallly seal the tortillas in plastic.

El Popo Tortilla Facility grew and prospered over the years. In 1983 Roberto Borrego, Sr. retired, and El Popo was sold in 1985. Now Roberto and Beatrice Borrego's oldest son, Roberto Jr. continues over seven decades of a family tradition, at his Adelita Tortilla and Tamale Factory.

In 2008, the Tortilla Industry Association Hall of Fame plaque was presented to Mr. Borrego in honor of the family business.

Adelita Tamales & Tortilla Factory can be found at (210) 733-5352 or at: www.adelitatamales.com/productsandservices.nxg

Making tortillas, 1925.

Making tamales, 1940s.

You Tube Tamales:
For making masa, tune in to YouTube to see the
Culinary Institute of America in San Antonio, Texas
with Chef Iliana de la Vega at:
http://www.youtube.com/watch?v=1778i23errM&feature=related

Las Tres Comadres

Ellen Riojas Clark, Ph.D.

Dr. Ellen Riojas Clark, born in San Antonio, is a graduate of Trinity University, UTSA, the University of Texas at Austin, and of many *tamaladas*. As Professor of Bicultural Bilingual Studies at the University of Texas-San Antonio, she has published over eighty academic articles. Ellen served as Educational Content Director for the Scholastic PBS children's cartoon series *Maya and Miguel* and claims the title of *Abuela Elena* on the series. Dr. Clark's contributions to the cultural life of San Antonio have been recognized with the *La Prensa* Outstanding Women in Action Award, the San Antonio Women's Hall of Fame, the Yellow Rose of Texas, and coronation as Queen *Huevo* for San Anto Cultural Center. She is one of the authors of *Las Dos Abuelas*, a *San Antonio Express-News* column on books and travel. Ellen has been featured in several documentaries— *Huipiles: Fabric of Identity; Latino Leaders, In Search of Racial Justice; Nachos, Tequila* and more; and *Hollydays*, where you can see her every Christmas, making her famous tamales. She and Hector are parents of two engineer daughters and four granddaughters. Her idea of heaven is a giant tamalada with chicken and *rajas* tamales, all her *comadres*, and a glass of champagne, whether from a $5 or a $150 bottle.

Carmen Tafolla, Ph.D.

Dr. Carmen Tafolla grew up in the west side *barrios* of San Antonio, Texas, west of the *matanzas*, south of the *molinos*, and north of *la labor de helote*. Tafolla is the author of more than fifteen books, including *The Holy Tortilla and a Pot of Beans, What Can You Do with a Paleta?, Fiesta Babies* and many others, and has been awarded the 2010 Américas Award, the Tomás Rivera Mexican-American Book Award (2009 and 2010), two International Latino Book Awards, the 2010 Charlotte Zolotow Award for best children's picture book writing, and the 1999 Art of Peace Award for "writing which contributes to peace, justice, and human understanding." She has performed her one-woman show in London, Madrid, Mexico City, Norway, Germany, Canada, New Zealand, Ireland, and throughout the United States. Dr. Tafolla teaches at the University of Texas-San Antonio, and is blessed with a home where her 92-year-old mother, her activist/scholar/husband Dr. Ernesto Bernal, her three children Mari, Israel and Ariana, grandson Anthony, and many *primos* and friends provide the constant *locura sabrosa* of a *tamalada*. Her favorite tamales are a tie between the green corn tamales made from low-fat mozzarella and canola oil by the *señora* in Flagstaff, or the tamales *de helote* her *tías* used to wrap in fresh, green shucks.

Thelma Ortíz-Muraida

An accomplished designer and artist, Ortíz-Muraida created the cover design for *The Holy Tortilla and a Pot of Beans* and designed the cover and illustrations for *Curandera* and *Sonnets to Human Beings/ Sonnete an Menschen*. She has also illustrated several articles for *National Association for the Education of Young Children* and the *Saguaro* journal. Her latest work in illustration is a children's picture book, *Clara and the Curandera,* by Monica Brown (Piñata Books, 2011.) Her unique combination of skills enable her to work across a broad range of design media, from print publications and illustration to exhibit and environmental designs. Currently she is teaching art and conducts workshops in *repujado*—the fine art of metal embossing. Her visual interpretations of typical tablecloths from San Antonio's Mexican kitchens, stylized *hojas de tamal*, and echoes of corn in its many forms create a unique backdrop and eloquent book design that put a crowning touch on this collaboration of *comadres* to feed the *pueblo*.

Acknowledgments

This edition would not have been possible without the tireless and artistically brilliant work of Thelma Ortiz-Muraida, the inspiration and *ánimo* of Olga Kauffman, the selflessness and optimism of David González, and the decisive support of Delicious Tamales. We would also like to offer thanks to Bryce Milligan for his generosity and assistance in the basics of book creation, to Rolando Briseño for so kindly allowing us to use his artwork on the cover, and to ALL the tamaleras who came before us, and who work beside us in this labor of love.

Wings Press was founded in 1975 by Joanie Whitebird and Joseph F. Lomax, both deceased, as "an informal association of artists and cultural mythologists dedicated to the preservation of the literature of the nation of Texas." Publisher, editor and designer since 1995, Bryce Milligan has been honored to carry on and expand that mission to include the finest in American writing—meaning *all* of the Americas, without commercial considerations clouding the choice to publish or not to publish.

Wings Press attempts to produce multicultural books, chapbooks, e-books, CDs, DVDs and broadsides that, we hope, enlighten the human spirit and enliven the mind. Everyone ever associated with Wings has been or is a writer; we know well that writing is a transformational art form capable of changing the world, primarily by allowing us to glimpse something of each other's souls. Good writing is innovative, insightful, and interesting. But most of all it is honest.

Likewise, Wings Press is committed to treating the planet itself as a partner. Thus the press uses as much recycled material as possible, from the paper on which the books are printed to the boxes in which they are shipped.

As Robert Dana wrote in *Against the Grain,* "Small press publishing is personal publishing. In essence, it's a matter of personal vision, personal taste and courage, and personal friendships." Welcome to our world.